The Wiersbe
BIBLE STUDY SERIES

The Wiersbe
BIBLE STUDY SERIES

JOSHUA

Putting God's
Power to
Work in
Your Life

DAVID C COOK

transforming lives together

THE WIERSBE BIBLE STUDY SERIES: JOSHUA
Published by David C Cook
4050 Lee Vance Drive
Colorado Springs, CO 80918 U.S.A.

Integrity Music Limited, a Division of David C Cook
Brighton, East Sussex BN1 2RE, England

The graphic circle C logo is a registered trademark of David C Cook.

Unless otherwise noted, all Scripture quotations in this study are taken from the
Holy Bible, New International Version of the Bible®, NIV®. Copyright © 1973, 1978,
1984 by Biblica, Inc.™ Used by permission of Zondervan. All rights reserved. www.
zondervan.com. Scripture quotations marked KJV are taken from the King James Version
of the Bible. (Public Domain); and NKJV are taken from the New King James Version.
Copyright © 1982 by Thomas Nelson, Inc. Used by permission. All rights reserved.

In the *Be Strong* excerpts, unless otherwise noted, all Scripture
quotations are taken from the King James Version of the Bible.

All excerpts taken from *Be Strong,* second edition, published by
David C Cook in 2010 © 1993 Warren W. Wiersbe, ISBN 978-1-4347-6637-3.

ISBN 978-1-4347-0232-6
eISBN 978-0-7814-0696-3

© 2011 Warren W. Wiersbe

The Team: Steve Parolini, Karen Lee-Thorp,
Amy Kiechlin Konyndyk, Sarah Schultz, Jack Campbell, Karen Athen
Series Cover Design: John Hamilton Design
Cover Photo: Veer DVP4973225

Printed in the United States of America
First Edition 2011

9 10 11 12 13 14 15 16 17 18

022321

Contents

Introduction to Joshua

Soldiers

The church needs the message of the book of Joshua more than ever before. We're living in a day of reproach and defeat, and the church is no longer "clear as the sun, and terrible as an army with banners" (Song 6:10 KJV). We look more like prisoners of war.

Whether we like it or not, God's people are expected to be soldiers. At least Paul thought so: "You therefore must endure hardship as a good soldier of Jesus Christ. No one engaged in warfare entangles himself with the affairs of this life, that he may please him who enlisted him as a soldier" (2 Tim. 2:3–4 NKJV).

The book of Joshua tells us how to be victorious soldiers and how to claim our rich, spiritual inheritance in Jesus Christ. It tells us how to be strong and courageous as we face our enemies and march forward to claim new territory for the Lord.

New Beginnings

The book of Joshua is the book of new beginnings for the people of God, and many believers today need a new beginning. After forty years of wandering in the wilderness, Israel claimed their inheritance and enjoyed the blessings of the land that God had prepared for them, "as the days of heaven upon the earth" (Deut. 11:21 KJV). That's the kind of life God wants us to experience today. Jesus Christ, our Joshua, wants to lead us in conquest now and share with us all the treasures of His wonderful inheritance. He has "blessed us with all spiritual blessings" (Eph. 1:3 KJV), but too often we live like defeated paupers.

Conquerors

The leading person in the book of Joshua is not Joshua but the Lord Jehovah, the God of Joshua and of Israel. In all that Joshua did by faith, he desired to glorify the Lord. When the Jews crossed the Jordan River, Joshua reminded them that the living God was among them and would overcome their enemies (Josh. 3:10). Through Israel's obedience, Joshua wanted all the people of the earth to know the Lord and fear Him (4:23–24). In his "farewell addresses" to the leaders (chap. 23) and to the nation (chap. 24), Joshua gave God all the glory for what Israel had accomplished under his leadership.

As you look at your life and the life of the church where you fellowship, do you see yourself and your fellow believers wandering in the wilderness or conquering in the Promised Land?

—Warren W. Wiersbe

How to Use This Study

This study is designed for both individual and small-group use. We've divided it into eight lessons—each references one or more chapters in Warren W. Wiersbe's commentary *Be Strong* (second edition, David C Cook, 2010). While reading *Be Strong* is not a prerequisite for going through this study, the additional insights and background Wiersbe offers can greatly enhance your study experience.

The **Getting Started** questions at the beginning of each lesson offer you an opportunity to record your first thoughts and reactions to the study text. This is an important step in the study process as those "first impressions" often include clues about what it is your heart is longing to discover.

The bulk of the study is found in the **Going Deeper** questions. These dive into the Bible text and, along with helpful excerpts from Wiersbe's commentary, help you examine not only the original context and meaning of the verses but also modern application.

Looking Inward narrows the focus down to your personal story. These intimate questions can be a bit uncomfortable at times, but don't shy away from honesty here. This is where you are asked to stand before the mirror of God's Word and look closely at what you see. It's the place to take a good look at yourself in light of the lesson and search for ways in which you can grow in faith.

Going Forward is the place where you can commit to paper those things you want or need to do in order to better live out the discoveries you made in the Looking Inward section. Don't skip or skim through this. Take the time to really consider what practical steps you might take to move closer to Christ. Then share your thoughts with a trusted friend who can act as an encourager and accountability partner.

Finally, there is a brief **Seeking Help** section to close the lesson. This is a reminder for you to invite God into your spiritual-growth process. If you choose to write out a prayer in this section, come back to it as you work through the lesson and continue to seek the Holy Spirit's guidance as you discover God's will for your life.

Tips for Small Groups

A small group is a dynamic thing. One week it might seem like a group of close-knit friends. The next it might seem more like a group of uncomfortable strangers. A small-group leader's role is to read these subtle changes and adjust the tone of the discussion accordingly.

Small groups need to be safe places for people to talk openly. It is through shared wrestling with difficult life issues that some of the greatest personal growth is discovered. But in order for the group to feel safe, participants need to know it's okay *not* to share sometimes. Always invite honest disclosure, but never force someone to speak if he or she isn't comfortable doing so. (A savvy leader will follow up later with a group member who isn't comfortable sharing in a group setting to see if a one-on-one discussion is more appropriate.)

Have volunteers take turns reading excerpts from Scripture or from the commentary. The more each person is involved even in the mundane tasks, the more they'll feel comfortable opening up in more meaningful ways.

The leader should watch the clock and keep the discussion moving. Sometimes there may be more Going Deeper questions than your group can cover in your available time. If you've had a fruitful discussion, it's okay to move on without finishing everything. And if you think the group is getting bogged down on a question or has taken off on a tangent, you can simply say, "Let's go on to question 5." Be sure to save at least ten to fifteen minutes for the Going Forward questions.

Finally, soak your group meetings in prayer—before you begin, during as needed, and always at the end of your time together.

Called to Lead
(JOSHUA 1)

Before you begin ...
- *Pray for the Holy Spirit to reveal truth and wisdom as you go through this lesson.*
- *Read Joshua 1. This lesson references chapter 2 in* Be Strong. *It will be helpful for you to have your Bible and a copy of the commentary available as you work through this lesson.*

Getting Started

From the Commentary

Twice during my years of ministry, I've been chosen to succeed distinguished and godly leaders and carry on their work. I can assure you that it wasn't easy to follow well-known Christians who sacrificially poured years of their lives into successful ministries. I can identify with Joshua when he stepped into Moses' sandals and discovered how big they were!

When I succeeded D. B. Eastep as pastor of Calvary Baptist Church in Covington, Kentucky, I remember how his widow and his son encouraged me and assured me of their support. I recall one of the deacons, George Evans, coming to the church office to tell me he would do anything to help me, "including washing your car and polishing your shoes." I never asked George to do either of those things, but his words expressed the encouraging attitude of all the church staff and leaders. I felt like a raw recruit taking the place of a seasoned veteran, and I needed all the help I could get! ...

What a new leader needs is not advice but encouragement. "To encourage" literally means "to put heart into." General Andrew Jackson said "one man with courage makes a majority," and he was right. As God's people today face the challenges that God gives us, we would do well to learn from the threefold encouragement found in this chapter.

—*Be Strong,* pages 29–30

1. What encouragement does Joshua get in this first chapter? How is this same encouragement applicable to today's leaders?

2. Choose one verse or phrase from Joshua 1 that stands out to you. This could be something you're intrigued by, something that makes you uncomfortable, something that puzzles you, something that resonates with you, or just something you want to examine further. Write that here.

Going Deeper

From the Commentary

Leaders don't lead forever, even godly leaders like Moses. There comes a time in every ministry when God calls for a new beginning with a new generation and new leadership. Except for Joshua and Caleb, the old generation of Jews had perished during the nation's wanderings in the wilderness, and Joshua was commissioned to lead the new generation into a new challenge: entering and conquering the Promised Land. "God buries His workmen, but His work goes on." It was God who had chosen Joshua, and everybody in Israel knew that he was their new leader.

Over the years I've seen churches and parachurch ministries flounder and almost destroy themselves in futile attempts to embalm the past and escape the future. Their theme song was, "As it was in the beginning, so shall it ever be, world without end." Often I've prayed with and for godly Christian leaders who were criticized, persecuted, and attacked simply because, like Joshua, they had a divine commission to lead a ministry into new fields of conquest, but the people would not follow. More than one pastor has been offered as a sacrificial lamb because he dared to suggest that the church make some changes.

—*Be Strong,* page 30

3. What does Joshua 1 have to say about new leadership? What are the challenges Joshua faced as he became a new leader? How are these like or unlike the challenges new leaders encounter today? How did Joshua approach his new role?

From the Commentary

A wise leader doesn't completely abandon the past but builds on it as he or she moves toward the future. Moses is mentioned fifty-seven times in the book of Joshua, evidence that Joshua respected Moses and what he had done for Israel. Joshua worshipped the same God that Moses had worshipped, and he obeyed the same Word that Moses had given to the nation. There was continuity from one leader to the next, but there wasn't always conformity, for each leader is different and must maintain his or her individuality. Twice in these verses Moses is called God's servant, but Joshua was also the servant of God (24:29). The important thing is not the servant but the Master.

—*Be Strong,* page 31

4. How did Joshua honor both Moses and God in his new role as leader? What are the risks and dangers of not showing honor to a previous leader? Explain.

More to Consider: In Joshua 1:1, Joshua is called "Moses' aide" (NIV) or "Moses' minister" (KJV). What's the significance of mentioning Joshua's title? (See Ex. 24:13; 33:11; Num. 11:28; Deut. 1:38.)

From the History Books

One of the most well-known military leaders in U.S. history is General George S. Patton. While highly regarded for his leadership during World War II, he was also quite a controversial figure. His no-nonsense style of leadership was lauded by many but questioned by others who decried his lack of compassion for soldiers suffering from battle fatigue. He was a bold, colorful figure who thought highly of himself and had little patience but ended up earning many awards for his military service.

5. What made Patton a great leader? What is it about leaders like Patton that intrigues us? How does a leader like Patton compare with leaders in the biblical narrative, such as Joshua? How do today's military leaders compare and contrast with Joshua? What lessons could today's leaders take from Joshua?

From the Commentary

> God commissioned Joshua to achieve three things: lead
> the people into the land, defeat the enemy, and claim the
> inheritance. God could have sent an angel to do this, but
> He chose to use a man and give him the power he needed
> to get the job done. As we have already seen, Joshua is a
> type of Jesus Christ, the Captain of our salvation (Heb.
> 2:10), who has won the victory and now shares His spiri-
> tual inheritance with us.
>
> —*Be Strong,* page 32

6. Read Joshua 1:3–6. What are the three promises God gives Joshua?
What is significant about the fact that God doesn't offer explanations for
His plans? What role does faith play in this interaction between God and
Joshua? How does it apply to leadership today?

From the Commentary

> Before God could fulfill His promises, however, Joshua
> had to exercise faith and "be strong and of a good courage"

(1:6). Divine sovereignty is not a substitute for human responsibility. God's sovereign Word is an encouragement to God's servants to believe God and obey His commands. As Charles Spurgeon put it in the *Metropolitan Tabernacle Pulpit*, Joshua "was not to use the promise as a couch upon which his indolence might luxuriate, but as a girdle wherewith to gird up his loins for future activity." In short, God's promises are prods, not pillows.

—*Be Strong*, page 34

7. What did it mean that Joshua needed to be "strong and courageous"? What obstacles could he have expected to face as he followed God's commands? How did Joshua take hold of God's promises? How do believers hold on to God's promises today?

From the Commentary

It's one thing to say to a leader, "Be strong! Be very courageous!" and quite something else to enable him to do it. Joshua's strength and courage would come from meditating on the Word of God, believing its promises, and obeying its precepts. This was the counsel Moses had given to all the people (Deut. 11:1–9), and now God was applying it specifically to Joshua.

—*Be Strong,* pages 34–35

8. Read Joshua 1:7–8. What is the encouragement from God's written Word that Joshua could count on? What is our encouragement from God's written Word today? How do we receive that encouragement?

More to Consider: Read Luke 1:37. How are Gabriel's words to Mary similar to God's words to Joshua? How do we embrace the truth of God's commands today?

From the Commentary

Though he trusted God for a miracle, Joshua still had to prepare for the everyday necessities of life. In modern armies the Quartermaster Corps sees to it that the soldiers have food and other necessities of life, but Israel didn't have a Quartermaster Corps. Each family and clan had to provide its own food. The manna was still falling each morning (Ex. 16) and wouldn't stop until Israel was in their land (Josh. 5:11–12). But it was important that the people stayed strong because they were about to begin a series of battles for possession of their Promised Land.

—*Be Strong,* page 37

9. What did Joshua say to his leaders? What does this tell us about his confidence in God's promises? What does it tell us about the role of leaders in encouraging others?

From the Commentary

The pronoun "they" in Joshua 1:16–18 probably refers to all the officers Joshua had addressed and not to the leaders of the two and a half tribes alone. What an encouragement they were to their new leader!

To begin with, they encouraged him by assuring him of their complete obedience (vv. 16–17a). "Command us and we will obey! Send us and we will go!" These officers had no hidden agendas, and they asked for no concessions. They would obey *all* his commands and go *wherever* he would send them. We could use that kind of commitment in the church today! Too many times we are like the men described in Luke 9:57–62, each of whom put something personal ahead of following the Lord.…

They encouraged Joshua by assuring him that their obedience was a matter of life or death (v. 18). They took his leadership and their responsibilities seriously.…

Finally, they encouraged him by reminding him of the Word of God (v. 18b). Moses told Joshua to "be ye of good courage" when he sent him and the other men into Canaan to spy out the land (Num. 13:20).

—*Be Strong,* pages 39–40

10. Why was encouragement from Joshua's officers significant to his leadership ability? What does it say about Joshua? About the people he surrounded himself with to help him lead? What does this tell us about leadership today?

Looking Inward

Take a moment to reflect on all that you've explored thus far in this study of Joshua 1. Review your notes and answers and think about how each of these things matters in your life today.

Tips for Small Groups: To get the most out of this section, form pairs or trios and have group members take turns answering these questions. Be honest and as open as you can in this discussion, but most of all, be encouraging and supportive of others. Be sensitive to those who are going through particularly difficult times and don't press for people to speak if they're uncomfortable doing so.

11. Have you ever taken over a leadership position from someone else? If so, what was that experience like? How did you honor the previous leader? How did you establish yourself as the new leader? What challenges did you face? How did you respond to those challenges?

12. What are the sources you turn to for support when called to take on a new responsibility? Where do you find encouragement? How do you deal with discouragement? What role does God's Word play in your leadership development?

13. What are ways you encourage other leaders today? How does this affect your relationship with those leaders? How can your encouragement help other leaders succeed? Why is this important?

Going Forward

14. Think of one or two things you have learned that you'd like to work on in the coming week. Remember that this is all about quality, not quantity. It's better to work on one specific area of life and do it well than to work on many and do poorly (or to be so overwhelmed that you simply don't try).

Do you need to learn how to trust God's promises? Do you want to learn how to be a more encouraging leader? Be specific. Go back through Joshua 1 and put a star next to the phrase or verse that is most encouraging to you. Consider memorizing this verse.

Real-Life Application Ideas: Consider the areas of your life where you're called to be a leader. This might be at work, home, church, or in other areas. It might be formal leadership or just taking initiative to get something done. Take a few minutes to evaluate your leadership in each arena. How are you being encouraged? How are you encouraging others? What role does God's Word play in your leadership? How are you trusting God's promises? As you evaluate all of these areas, look for opportunities for improvement and commit to making those changes.

Seeking Help

15. Write a prayer below (or simply pray one in silence), inviting God to work on your mind and heart in those areas you've noted above. Be honest about your desires and fears.

Notes for Small Groups:

- *Look for ways to put into practice the things you wrote in the Going Forward section. Talk with other group members about your ideas and commit to being accountable to one another.*

- *During the coming week, ask the Holy Spirit to continue to reveal truth to you from what you've read and studied.*

- *Before you start the next lesson, read Joshua 2—4. For more in-depth lesson preparation, read chapters 3 and 4, "A Convert in Canaan" and "Forward by Faith," in* Be Strong.

Spies and Truth
(JOSHUA 2—4)

Before you begin …
- *Pray for the Holy Spirit to reveal truth and wisdom as you go through this lesson.*
- *Read Joshua 2—4. This lesson references chapters 3–4 in* Be Strong. *It will be helpful for you to have your Bible and a copy of the commentary available as you work through this lesson.*

Getting Started

From the Commentary

It's remarkable how God in His grace uses people we might think could never become His servants. "But God has chosen the foolish things of the world to put to shame the wise, and God has chosen the weak things of the world to put to shame the things which are mighty; and the base things of the world and the things which are despised God has chosen, and the things which are not, to bring to nothing the things that are, that no flesh should glory in His presence" (1 Cor. 1:27–29 NKJV). Jesus was the "friend of publicans and sinners" (Luke 7:34), and He wasn't ashamed to have a former prostitute in His family tree!

—*Be Strong,* page 47

1. Review Joshua 2:1–7. How are Rahab's actions evidence of faith? Why is it significant that the Bible includes this story? What's unique about it when compared to the rest of the biblical narrative? What does this tell us about how God brings about His plans? About who can be used by God to bring about those plans?

More to Consider: Read Proverbs 12:22. Obviously, lying is wrong. What made Rahab's lies "okay" in this story? Does this mean God is saying lying is okay sometimes? Why or why not?

2. Choose one verse or phrase from Joshua 2—4 that stands out to you. This could be something you're intrigued by, something that makes you uncomfortable, something that puzzles you, something that resonates with you, or just something you want to examine further. Write that here.

Going Deeper

From the Commentary

Faith is only as good as its object. Some people have faith in faith and think that just by *believing* they can make great things happen. Others have faith in lies, which is not faith at all but superstition. I once heard a psychologist say that the people in a support group "must have some kind of faith, even if it's faith in the soft drink machine." But faith is only as good as its object. How much help can you get from a soft drink machine, especially after you've run out of money?

D. Martyn Lloyd-Jones reminds us that "faith shows itself in the whole personality." True saving faith isn't just a feat of intellectual gymnastics by which we convince ourselves that something is true that really isn't true. Nor is it merely a stirring of the emotions that gives us a false sense of confidence that God will do what we *feel* He will do. Nor is it a courageous act of the will whereby we jump off the pinnacle of the temple and expect God to rescue us (Matt. 4:5–7). True saving faith involves "the whole personality": the mind is instructed, the emotions are stirred, and the will then acts in obedience to God.

—*Be Strong,* pages 48–49

3. Review Joshua 2:8–11. What does it mean that "faith is only as good as its object"? What was the object of Rahab's faith? Why did she have such

faith in God? How did this affect the decisions she made when the spies arrived?

From the Commentary

> "The LORD your God, he is God in heaven above, and in earth beneath" (Josh. 2:11). What a confession of faith from the lips of a woman whose life had been imprisoned in pagan idolatry! She believed in *one God,* not in the multitude of gods that populated the heathen temples. She believed He was a *personal* God ("your God"), who would work on behalf of those who trusted Him. She believed He was *the God of Israel,* who would give the land to His people. This God whom she trusted was not limited to one nation or one land, but was *the God of heaven and earth.* Rahab believed in a great and awesome God!

> Our confidence that we are God's children comes from the witness of the Word of God before us and the witness of the Spirit of God within us (1 John 5:9–13). However, the assurance of salvation isn't based only on what we know from the Bible or how we feel in our hearts. It's also based on how we live, for if there hasn't been a change

in our behavior, then it's doubtful that we've truly been born again (2 Cor. 5:21; James 2:14–26). It isn't enough to say "Lord, Lord!" We must obey what He tells us to do (Matt. 7:21–27). Rahab's obedience gave evidence of a changed life.

—Be Strong, page 50

4. In what ways was Rahab's conversion an act of God's grace? What does this story teach us about God's grace? How did Rahab's obedience reveal the character of her heart?

From Today's World

If you go to the movies or watch TV or read popular literature these days, you will undoubtedly run into plots where lies or deceit play a critical role. In many cases, lies are treated as "par for the course" in relationships—and sometimes are even directly or indirectly celebrated because they lead to a happy ending. Secrets and lies are nothing new, but their ubiquity in modern media certainly is notable.

5. Why do you think lies are used so often in today's movie, TV, or book storylines? What is the intrigue of lying as a plot element? How do these

shows attempt to redeem lies and deceit? How is this different from the role of lies in Rahab's story?

From the Commentary

> Rahab wasn't concerned only about her own welfare, for once she had personally experienced the grace and mercy of God, she was burdened to rescue her family. After Andrew met the Lord Jesus, he shared the good news with his brother Simon and brought him to Jesus (John 1:35–42). The cleansed leper went home and told everybody he met what Jesus had done for him (Mark 1:40–45). "The fruit of the righteous is a tree of life; and he that winneth souls is wise" (Prov. 11:30).
>
> —*Be Strong,* page 51

6. Why was Rahab concerned about her family? (See Joshua 2:11–14.) What assurances did she seek from the spies? What assurance did she get? Why was this important?

More to Consider: Read about the covenant in Joshua 2:15–24. Then read about a few other divine covenants: Genesis 2:16–17; Exodus 19—20; 2 Samuel 7; Jeremiah 31:31; Matthew 26:28; Hebrews 12:24. What is similar about each of these covenants? What does a covenant really mean?

From the Commentary

> The spies instructed Rahab to hang a scarlet rope out of the window of her house, which was built into the wall (Josh. 2:18). This scarlet rope would identify the "house of safety" to the army of Israel when they came to take the city. The color of the rope is significant, for it reminds us of blood. Just as the blood on the doorposts in Egypt marked a house that the angel of death was to pass over (Ex. 12:1–13), so the scarlet rope marked a house on the Jericho wall whose occupants the Jewish soldiers were to protect. Rahab let the men down from the window with that rope and kept it in the window from that hour. This was the "sure sign" of the covenant that she had asked for (Josh. 2:12–23).
>
> —*Be Strong,* page 53

7. In what ways is the red rope a symbol of faith in God? How is it similar to the blood on the doorposts when the Israelites were captive in Egypt? What is the role of symbols like this red rope in the life of a believer? What happens when we put our faith in the symbol instead of what it represents?

From the Commentary

We've just examined the faith of an individual, Rahab, and now the focus in the book of Joshua moves to the faith of an entire nation. As you study, keep in mind that this book deals with much more than ancient history—what God did centuries ago for the Jews. It's about your life and the life of the church today—what God wants to do here and now for those who trust Him. The book of Joshua is about the victory of faith and the glory that comes to God when His people trust and obey. British Prime Minister Benjamin Disraeli said, "The world was never conquered by intrigue; it was conquered by faith." ...

In Joshua 3 and 4, God illustrates for us three essentials for moving ahead by faith and claiming all that He has for us....

The first of these is the word of faith (3:1–13).

As the nation waited by the Jordan River, the people must have wondered what Joshua planned to do. He certainly wouldn't ask them to swim the river or ford it, because the river was at flood stage (3:15). They couldn't construct enough boats or rafts to transport more than a million people over the water to the other side. Besides, that approach would make them perfect targets for their enemies. What would their new leader do?

—*Be Strong*, pages 57–59

8. What was the "word of faith" that Joshua counted on when his people reached the Jordan? Where did he get this word? Why is it that "faith" and "waiting" intersect so often in God's plan? Why is waiting so hard? What role did Joshua's character (and his own faith in God) play in helping his people trust God's unrevealed plan?

From the Commentary

The second essential for moving ahead by faith and claiming all that God has for us is the walk of faith (3:14–17).

During most of the year, the Jordan River was about a hundred feet wide, but at the spring flood season, the river overflowed its banks and became a mile wide. As soon as the priests bearing the ark put their feet into the river, the water stopped flowing and stood like a wall about twenty miles away upstream, near a city called Adam. It was a miracle of God in response to the faith of the people.

Unless we step out by faith (1:3) and "get our feet wet," we're not likely to make much progress in living for Christ and serving Him. Each step that the priests took opened the water before them until they were standing in the midst of the river on dry ground. They stood there as the people passed by, and when the whole nation had crossed, the priests walked to the shore and the flow of the water resumed.

When God opened the Red Sea, He used a strong wind that blew the whole night before (Ex. 14:21–22). This was not an accident, for the wind was the blast of God's nostrils (15:8). When Moses lifted his rod, the wind began to blow, and when he lowered the rod, the waters flowed back and drowned the Egyptian army (14:26–28). When Israel crossed the Jordan River, it was not the obedient arm of a leader that brought the miracle but the obedient feet of the people. Unless we are willing to step out by faith and obey His Word, God can never open the way for us.

—Be Strong, pages 63–64

9. How might God's earlier miracle at the Red Sea have helped the Israelites as they considered the obstacle of the Jordan River? How can both of these miracles help believers learn to trust God's leading today? What role did Joshua play in helping the Israelites move forward in God's plan? How is that similar to the role Christian leaders play today?

From the Commentary

The third essential for moving ahead by faith and claiming all that God has for us is the witness of faith (4:1–24).

The Lord was in control of all the activities at the Jordan River that day. He told the priests when to enter the river and when to leave and go to the other side. He told the water when to roll back and when to return. Both the water and the people obeyed Him, and everything worked out as God planned. It was a day that glorified the Lord and magnified His servant Joshua (v. 14).

Two heaps of stones were set up as memorials of Israel's crossing of the Jordan River: twelve stones at Gilgal (vv. 1–8, 10–24), and twelve stones in the midst of the river (v. 9). They were witnesses that God honors faith and works on behalf of those who trust Him.

—Be Strong, page 65

10. How does the witness of faith help believers who follow in the footsteps of those who saw God's great power? What are some of the witnesses of faith that today's Christians can look to for strength and confidence to move ahead? How can today's believers become witnesses of faith for the next generation?

Looking Inward

Take a moment to reflect on all that you've explored thus far in this study of Joshua 2—4. Review your notes and answers and think about how each of these things matters in your life today.

Tips for Small Groups: To get the most out of this section, form pairs or trios and have group members take turns answering these questions. Be honest and as open as you can in this discussion, but most of all, be encouraging and supportive of others. Be sensitive to those who are going through particularly difficult times and don't press for people to speak if they're uncomfortable doing so.

11. What about Rahab's story inspires you? In what ways can you relate to Rahab? What does her faith teach you about the breadth of God's grace? How have you experienced that grace?

12. In Rahab's story, lies were used to protect the spies. What does this tell you about Rahab? About how she understood what it means to trust God? In what ways have you acted like Rahab when responding to God's call on your life? Have you ever felt called to do something you normally wouldn't? How do you know when that tug is from God?

13. What are some obstacles you've encountered in your life that loom like the overflowing Jordan River? How did you respond when you first faced these obstacles? What role did trust in God play as you sought the way through (or around) them?

Going Forward

14. Think of one or two things you have learned that you'd like to work on in the coming week. Remember that this is all about quality, not quantity. It's better to work on one specific area of life and do it well than to work on many and do poorly (or to be so overwhelmed that you simply don't try).

Do you want to get your feet wet, acting on faith in God? Do you long to embrace God's grace, as Rahab did? Be specific. Go back through Joshua 2—4 and put a star next to the phrase or verse that is most encouraging to you. Consider memorizing this verse.

Real-Life Application Ideas: What is one "promised land" you're feeling led to these days? (This might be a career change or something to do with family, friends, or your community.) How do you know if this is something God wants for you or if it's something you simply want for yourself? Talk with wise friends about this and spend time in Scripture seeking God's will. Then note the obstacles in your way. Seek God's heart patiently in prayer and supplication as you listen for wisdom on how to move beyond these obstacles.

Seeking Help

15. Write a prayer below (or simply pray one in silence), inviting God to work on your mind and heart in those areas you've noted above. Be honest about your desires and fears.

Notes for Small Groups:

- *Look for ways to put into practice the things you wrote in the Going Forward section. Talk with other group members about your ideas and commit to being accountable to one another.*

- *During the coming week, ask the Holy Spirit to continue to reveal truth to you from what you've read and studied.*

- *Before you start the next lesson, read Joshua 5. For more in-depth lesson preparation, read chapter 5, "Preparing for Victory," in* Be Strong.

Higher Ways
(JOSHUA 5)

Before you begin ...
- *Pray for the Holy Spirit to reveal truth and wisdom as you go through this lesson.*
- *Read Joshua 5. This lesson references chapter 5 in* Be Strong. *It will be helpful for you to have your Bible and a copy of the commentary available as you work through this lesson.*

Getting Started

From the Commentary

The nation of Israel arrived safely on the other side of the Jordan River. Their crossing was a great miracle, and it sent a great message to the people of the land (5:1). The Canaanites were already afraid (2:9–11), and now their fears totally demoralized them.

You would have expected Joshua to mobilize the army immediately and attack Jericho. After all, the people of

Israel were united in following the Lord, and the people of the land were paralyzed by fear. From the human point of view, it was the perfect time for Joshua to act.

But God's thoughts and ways are higher than ours (Isa. 55:8–9), and Joshua was getting his orders from the Lord, not from the military experts. The nation crossed the river on the tenth day of the first month (Josh. 4:19). The events described in Joshua 5 took at least ten days, and then the people marched around Jericho for six more days. God waited over two weeks before giving His people their first victory in the land.

God's people must be *prepared* before they can be trusted with victory. The triumphant conquest of the land was to be the victory of God, not the victory of Israel or of Joshua.

—Be Strong, page 71

1. Why do you think God made the Israelites wait over two weeks before sending them into Jericho? How does this time of waiting test the people? The leadership? What message does this story have for God's people today? For leaders?

More to Consider: After triumphantly crossing the Jordan River, the nation paused at Gilgal while the men submitted to painful surgery. Why did God command this ritual at this time? (See Josh. 5:2–7.)

2. Choose one verse or phrase from Joshua 5 that stands out to you. This could be something you're intrigued by, something that makes you uncomfortable, something that puzzles you, something that resonates with you, or just something you want to examine further. Write that here.

Going Deeper

From the Commentary

Through the ritual of circumcision the Jews became a "marked people" because they belonged to the true and living God. This meant that they were under obligation to obey Him. The mark of the covenant reminded them that their bodies belonged to the Lord and were not to be used for sinful purposes. Israel was surrounded by nations that worshipped idols and included in their worship rituals that were sensual and degrading. The mark of the covenant reminded the Jews that they were a special people, a separated people, a holy nation (Ex. 19:5–6), and that they were to maintain purity in their marriages, their society, and their worship of God.

—*Be Strong,* page 72

3. Review Joshua 5:2–7. Why was it important for the Israelites to be "marked" by God? (See Ex. 19:5–6.) What does it mean to be a holy people? How do Christians identify themselves with God today? What are the "marks" of a Christian faith?

From the Commentary

This physical operation on the body was meant to be a symbol of a *spiritual operation on the heart.* "Therefore circumcise the foreskin of your heart, and be stiff-necked no longer" (Deut. 10:16 NKJV). No amount of external surgery can change the inner person. It's when we repent and turn to God for help that He can change our hearts and make us love and obey Him more. (See Rom. 2:25–29.)

But over the years, the Jews came to trust in the external *mark* of the covenant and not in the *God* of the covenant who wanted to make them a holy people.

—*Be Strong,* page 73

4. Why do you think the Jews came to trust the external mark of the covenant instead of the internal mark? How do believers do this today? How can we overcome the temptation to trust symbols rather than what they represent?

From Today's World

The importance of symbols varies greatly from one sect of Christianity to the next. For some, the symbols provide a quiet reminder of Jesus' sacrifice. For others, the symbols carry much more weight and are believed to accomplish cleansing, spiritual nourishment, and so on. Symbols aren't limited to religious belief systems, though. They're evident in everything from gangs to the military to corporate settings and anywhere else where people want to identify themselves as members of a certain group.

5. What are the benefits of outward symbols? What are the risks? Why do people want to identify themselves in certain groups? What do they

get out of this association? When does an outward symbol become more important than what it represents?

From the Commentary

> Israel was camped in enemy territory, just a few miles from Jericho. Now they were going to *temporarily disable every male in the nation,* including every soldier in the army! What a golden opportunity for the enemy to attack and wipe them out. (See Gen. 34.) It took faith for Joshua and the people to obey the Lord, but their obedience to the law was the secret of their success (Josh. 1:7–8). In their weakness they were made strong, and through faith and patience they inherited the promises (Heb. 6:12).
>
> —*Be Strong,* pages 73–74

6. Read Joshua 5:8. Why didn't the enemy attack during this time when the Israelite men were weakened? How might the Israelites have responded to Joshua's leadership during this time? What role did trust play in this situation? How does a leader earn the sort of trust that Joshua had with his men?

From the Commentary

> The word *Gilgal* is similar to the Hebrew word *galal*, which means "to roll." But what was "the reproach of Egypt"? Some suggest that this means their reproach for being slaves in Egypt, but it wasn't Israel's fault that the new pharaoh turned against them (Ex. 1:8ff.). The Jews were in Egypt because God had sent them there (Gen. 46:1–4), not because they were disobedient.
>
> It's also been suggested that "the reproach of Egypt" refers to the nation's shame because they had worshipped idols in Egypt (Ezek. 20:7–8; 23:3) and even during their wilderness wanderings (Amos 5:25–26; Acts 7:42–43). But that older generation was now dead, and the younger Israelites certainly shouldn't be blamed for the sins of their fathers. Furthermore, it's difficult for me to see the relationship between crossing the river, circumcision, and the Jews' idolatry in Egypt.
>
> I think that "the reproach of Egypt" refers to the ridicule of the enemy when Israel failed to trust God at Kadesh Barnea and enter the Promised Land.
>
> —*Be Strong,* pages 74–75

7. Why was it significant that God mentioned the "reproach of Egypt"? How does Joshua 5:9 help us to see God's hand in the Israelites' ongoing story?

From the Commentary

> "Forgetting those things which are behind" (Phil. 3:13)
> is wise counsel for most areas of life, but there are some
> things we must never forget. In his farewell address to
> the nation, Moses repeatedly commanded the Jews to
> remember that they were once slaves in Egypt and that
> the Lord had delivered them and made them His own
> people (Deut. 6:15; 15:15; 16:12; 24:18, 22). This great
> truth was embodied in their annual Passover Feast.
>
> —*Be Strong,* page 77

8. Read Joshua 5:10–12. Why was it important that the Israelites celebrated the Passover? What are the risks of not remembering the things of the past? How do we know what things we should remember and what should be forgotten? How do we celebrate remembering important biblical truths today?

More to Consider: Joshua 5:10–12 notes the end of God's provision of manna and therefore the promise of a new harvest in Canaan. Why was this significant in the Israelites' story? In what ways did Jesus compare Himself to both the manna (John 6:26–59) and the harvest (4:34–38; 12:20–28)?

From the Commentary

> Joshua had read in the book of the law what Moses had said to the Lord after Israel had made the golden calf: "If Your Presence does not go with us, do not bring us up from here" (Ex. 33:15 NKJV). The Lord had promised to be with Joshua just as He had been with Moses (Josh. 1:5), and now He reaffirmed that promise in a personal way. Like his predecessor, Joshua refused to move until he was sure the Lord's presence was with him.
>
> —*Be Strong*, page 79

9. How did Joshua reaffirm the Lord's presence? (See Josh. 5:13–15.) Why was this important to his leadership ability? How do believers today affirm God's presence?

From the Commentary

In Christian ministry great public victories are won in private as leaders submit to the Lord and receive their directions from Him. It's doubtful that anybody in the camp of Israel knew about their leader's meeting with the Lord, but that meeting made the difference between success and failure on the battlefield. The Chinese Bible teacher Watchman Nee wrote, "Not until we take the place of a servant can He take His place as Lord."

Joshua was reminded that he was *second in command.* Every father and mother, pastor, and Christian leader is second in command to the Lord Jesus Christ, and when we forget this fact, we start to move toward defeat and failure. The Lord came to Joshua that day, not just to help but *to lead.* "Without Me you can do nothing" (John 15:5 NKJV). Joshua was an experienced soldier, whom Moses had trained for leadership. Yet that was no guarantee of success. He needed the presence of the Lord God.

—*Be Strong,* pages 80–81

10. Read John 15:5. How does this verse apply to Joshua's situation? What does being "second in command" look like in practical terms? How do leaders submit to God? How does this submission reveal itself to followers?

Looking Inward

Take a moment to reflect on all that you've explored thus far in this study of Joshua 5. Review your notes and answers and think about how each of these things matters in your life today.

Tips for Small Groups: To get the most out of this section, form pairs or trios and have group members take turns answering these questions. Be honest and as open as you can in this discussion, but most of all, be encouraging and supportive of others. Be sensitive to those who are going through particularly difficult times and don't press for people to speak if they're uncomfortable doing so.

11. What are some of the things you've had to wait upon God for? Did you struggle with impatience? Explain. Why is it so difficult to trust God during times when nothing seems to be happening?

12. In what ways are you "marked" as a believer? How do the outward symbols reflect your inward truth? Have you ever put too much emphasis on the symbol instead of the truth? Explain.

13. The Israelites celebrated Passover to remember their rescue from captivity. What are some ways you celebrate what has brought you to this place in your faith? Do you do a good job of remembering God's role in your story? What could you do better?

Going Forward

14. Think of one or two things you have learned that you'd like to work on in the coming week. Remember that this is all about quality, not quantity. It's better to work on one specific area of life and do it well than to work on many and do poorly (or to be so overwhelmed that you simply don't try).

Do you need to learn how to wait on God? Be specific. Go back through Joshua 5 and put a star next to the phrase or verse that is most encouraging to you. Consider memorizing this verse.

Real-Life Application Ideas: The overarching theme of Joshua 5 is learning how to be spiritually prepared for the work you do. Think about your own work—not just your job, but also your role as friend, parent, volunteer. How do you prepare for this work spiritually? If you don't have a specific plan for your preparation, consider making one and sticking to it. You might include regular prayer, study, and conversation with spiritual leaders.

Seeking Help

15. Write a prayer below (or simply pray one in silence), inviting God to work on your mind and heart in those areas you've noted above. Be honest about your desires and fears.

Notes for Small Groups:

- *Look for ways to put into practice the things you wrote in the Going Forward section. Talk with other group members about your ideas and commit to being accountable to one another.*

- *During the coming week, ask the Holy Spirit to continue to reveal truth to you from what you've read and studied.*

- *Before you start the next lesson, read Joshua 6. For more in-depth lesson preparation, read chapter 6, "The Conquest Begins!" in* Be Strong.

The Battle
(JOSHUA 6)

Before you begin …
- *Pray for the Holy Spirit to reveal truth and wisdom as you go through this lesson.*
- *Read Joshua 6. This lesson references chapter 6 in* Be Strong. *It will be helpful for you to have your Bible and a copy of the commentary available as you work through this lesson.*

Getting Started

From the Commentary

> It's unfortunate that many of the "militant songs" of the church have been removed from some hymnals, apparently because the idea of warfare disturbs people and seems to contradict the words and works of Jesus Christ. But these zealous editors with scissors seem to have forgotten that the main theme of the Bible is God's holy warfare against Satan and sin. In Genesis 3:15, God declared war on Satan, and one day He will declare the victory when

Jesus comes as Conqueror to establish His kingdom (Rev. 19:11–21). *If you eliminate the militant side of the Christian faith, then you must abandon the cross, for it was on the cross that Jesus won the victory over sin and Satan* (Col. 2:13–15).

—*Be Strong,* pages 85–86

1. Why do you think many churches are uncomfortable with the military imagery in the Bible? What are some of the ways your church still uses this imagery? How can this imagery strengthen the church? What are the dangers of overemphasizing this imagery?

More to Consider: Read Paul's warning about the savage wolves that are ready to destroy the flock (Acts 20:28–29). How does this passage relate to the military themes in Joshua 6?

2. Choose one verse or phrase from Joshua 6 that stands out to you. This could be something you're intrigued by, something that makes you uncomfortable, something that puzzles you, something that resonates with you, or just something you want to examine further. Write that here.

Going Deeper

From the Commentary

> The Christian's warfare is not against flesh and blood, but against enemies in the spiritual realm (Eph. 6:10–18), and the weapons we use are spiritual (2 Cor. 10:3–6). Satan and his demonic armies use people to oppose and attack the church of God, and if we don't take our stand with Christ, *we've already lost the battle.* In the army of Jesus Christ there can be no neutrality. "He that is not with me is against me," said Jesus, and He spoke those words in the context of spiritual warfare (Matt. 12:24–30). Since the apostle Paul often used the military image to describe the Christian life, we dare not ignore the subject (Eph. 6:10ff.; 2 Tim. 2:1–4; Rom. 13:12; 1 Thess. 5:8).
>
> —*Be Strong,* page 86

3. The Old Testament is rife with stories of great battles between good and evil. What does God reveal about Himself through the battles described in Joshua? What are some examples of "battles" today that reveal the heart of God?

From the Commentary

> The Christian soldier stands in a position of guaranteed
> victory because Jesus Christ has already defeated every
> spiritual enemy (John 12:31). Jesus defeated Satan not
> only in the wilderness (Matt. 4:1–11), but also during His
> earthly ministry (12:22–29), on the cross (Col. 2:13–15),
> and in His resurrection and ascension (Eph. 1:19–23).
> As He intercedes for His people in heaven, He helps us
> mature and accomplish His will (Heb. 13:20–21), and "if
> God be for us, who can be against us?" (Rom. 8:31).
>
> —*Be Strong,* pages 86–87

4. Read Joshua 6:1–5. This passage tells us that the victory is assured
with God on our side. How might such assurance affect the way soldiers
approach the battle? Does this mean there won't be any suffering? Explain.
How is this truth evident also today when people encounter trials? What
does God's assurance of victory look like to those who are enduring pain?

From the History Books

If you look back at the history of wars on our planet, you'll find a few repeating themes. One is that most wars are sparked by a disagreement over land. Rather than work things out in a civilized, peaceful fashion, nations choose to battle for what they believe is rightfully theirs. Another common theme is fear. Nations operate frequently out of fear—fear of losing their power, significance, or meaning in the context of the larger world. A third common theme is lack of trust. If nations trusted each other, they could come to the table and talk through issues calmly. But a lack of trust leads to secrecy and espionage and often leads to fights over what may amount to nothing but misinformation.

5. What sort of battle were the Israelites' embroiled in at Jericho? What role did the desire for property play? Fear? Distrust? How are these factors significant in the battles we face around our world today? What role do they play in more domestic "battles," whether over politics or relationships? How did God step into the battle at Jericho to resolve all of these issues? How can He help us with the battles we face today?

From the Commentary

> It's possible that the Lord spoke the following words to
> Joshua when He confronted him at Jericho (5:13–15).
> The tense of the verb is important: *"I have given* Jericho
> into your hand" (6:2 NKJV, italics added). The victory had
> already been won! All Joshua and his people had to do
> was claim the promise and obey the Lord.
>
> —*Be Strong,* page 88

6. How did Joshua claim God's promise of victory? What makes a believer
today victorious? How do Christians become familiar with God's promises?
(See Josh. 1:8; Rom. 10:17.)

From the Commentary

> "By faith the walls of Jericho fell down, after they were
> compassed about seven days" (Heb. 11:30). "And this
> is the victory that has overcome the world—our faith"
> (1 John 5:4 NKJV).

Faith is not believing in spite of evidence, for the people of Israel had been given one demonstration after another proving that God's Word and God's power can be trusted.

—*Be Strong,* page 91

7. Read Joshua 6:6–16, 20. How were the Israelites' actions evidence of faith? What evidence did they have that God would deliver what He had promised? What evidence do we have today that God delivers on His promises? How does this inform our faith?

From the Commentary

The activities of the week were a test of the Jewish people's faith and patience. No doubt some of them were anxious to get on with the invasion so they could claim their inheritance and settle down to enjoy the rest God had promised them (Josh. 1:13). To some of them, it may have seemed a futile waste of time to devote an entire week to the taking of one city. Impatience was one of Israel's besetting sins, and God was helping them learn patient obedience, for it's through "faith and patience" that God's people inherit what He has promised (Heb. 6:12). *God is never in a hurry.* He knows what He's doing, and His timing is never off.

If the week's schedule was a test of their patience, the divine command of silence was a test of their self-control. People who can't control their tongues can't control their bodies (James 3:1–2), and what good are soldiers whose bodies are not disciplined? "Be still, and know that I am God" (Ps. 46:10). In the Christian life there's "a time to keep silence, and a time to speak" (Eccl. 3:7), and wise is the child of God who knows the difference.

—*Be Strong,* page 92

8. How did the people in Jericho respond to the march around their city? Why was the command of silence difficult for the Israelites? Why is it difficult to keep quiet in the face of great challenges? How did Jesus model this wisdom of knowing when to be quiet and when to speak? (See Isa. 53:7; Matt. 26:62–63; 27:14; Luke 23:9.)

More to Consider: The Holy Spirit directed the writer of Hebrews to use this event as one of the "by faith" examples (Heb. 11:30). In what ways was the fall of Jericho an encouragement to God's people?

From the Commentary

Let me quote Andrew Bonar's wise counsel: "Let us be as watchful after the victory as before the battle." Because one soldier didn't heed this warning, Israel's next challenge in Canaan turned out to be a humiliating defeat. Joshua gave the soldiers four instructions to obey after they had taken the city. The first two were:

(1) Devote the entire city to God (Josh. 6:17–19). This meant that everything was dedicated to the Lord—the people, the houses, the animals, and all the spoils of war—and He could do with it whatever He pleased.…

(2) Rescue Rahab and her family (Josh. 6:22–23, 25–26).…

God saved and protected Rahab because of her faith (Heb. 11:31), and because she led her family to trust in Jehovah, they were also saved.

—*Be Strong*, pages 93–94

9. Review Joshua 6:17–19, 21–27. Why did Joshua give the instruction to devote the entire city to God? What did he mean by that? How are we to devote our communities to God today? Why did Joshua single out Rahab and her family? What lesson is there in this directive for us today?

From the Commentary

Joshua gave the soldiers four instructions to obey after they had taken the city. The last two were:

(3) Destroy the people (Josh. 6:21). It disturbs some people that God commanded every living thing in Jericho to be killed. Isn't our God a God of mercy? After all, it's one thing for the Jews to kill the enemy soldiers, but why kill women, children, and even animals? …

(4) Burn the city (Josh. 6:24). "Thy God is a consuming fire" was spoken by Moses in Deuteronomy 4:24 long before it was quoted by the Holy Spirit in Hebrews 12:29.

—*Be Strong,* pages 95, 97

10. Why did God direct Joshua to destroy the people and burn the city after the Israelites' victory? What message was He giving to the Israelites? What message is He giving us today in this story?

Looking Inward

Take a moment to reflect on all that you've explored thus far in this study of Joshua 6. Review your notes and answers and think about how each of these things matters in your life today.

Tips for Small Groups: To get the most out of this section, form pairs or trios and have group members take turns answering these questions. Be honest and as open as you can in this discussion, but most of all, be encouraging and supportive of others. Be sensitive to those who are going through particularly difficult times and don't press for people to speak if they're uncomfortable doing so.

11. Are you comfortable with the military imagery in the Bible? Why or why not? What are some of the battles you've been facing lately? In what ways are you trusting God for victory in these battles? What would victory look like to you? What might it look like to God?

12. The Israelites had to confront their fears when preparing for the battle at Jericho. What are some fears you're wrestling with today? How do these fears affect your ability to live the life God desires for you? How can God's

assurance help you overcome your fears? What are other ways you can confront your fears?

13. Do you have difficulty knowing when to be quiet and when to speak up? Explain. How would you have felt about God's command for silence during the Jericho story? How has staying silent served you well in the past? How has speaking up when you should be quiet gotten you into trouble? Where can you seek wisdom for when to be quiet and when to speak up?

Going Forward

14. Think of one or two things you have learned that you'd like to work on in the coming week. Remember that this is all about quality, not quantity. It's better to work on one specific area of life and do it well than to work on many and do poorly (or to be so overwhelmed that you simply don't try).

Do you want to cultivate trust in God as you face something you fear? Be specific. Go back through Joshua 6 and put a star next to the phrase or verse that is most encouraging to you. Consider memorizing this verse.

Real-Life Application Ideas: A big theme in the battle of Jericho is patience. Think about one or more long-term goals you have in life— whether work- or family-related. For example, this could be a desire to own your own business someday or move your family to a new home. Now think about the steps it will take to make your goal happen. Where does patience fit into the plan? When should you act and when should you wait? How might "be patient" work as an action step in your plan? Work on that plan. Don't forget to spend time in patient prayer and counsel with others as you work toward your goals.

Seeking Help

15. Write a prayer below (or simply pray one in silence), inviting God to work on your mind and heart in those areas you've noted above. Be honest about your desires and fears.

Notes for Small Groups:
- *Look for ways to put into practice the things you wrote in the Going Forward section. Talk with other group members about your ideas and commit to being accountable to one another.*
- *During the coming week, ask the Holy Spirit to continue to reveal truth to you from what you've read and studied.*
- *Before you start the next lesson, read Joshua 7—8. For more in-depth lesson preparation, read chapters 7 and 8, "Defeat in the Land of Victory" and "Turning Defeat into Victory," in* Be Strong.

Defeat
(JOSHUA 7—8)

Before you begin …
- *Pray for the Holy Spirit to reveal truth and wisdom as you go through this lesson.*
- *Read Joshua 7—8. This lesson references chapters 7–8 in* Be Strong. *It will be helpful for you to have your Bible and a copy of the commentary available as you work through this lesson.*

Getting Started

From the Commentary

The ominous word *but* that introduces Joshua 7 is a signal that things are going to change, for Joshua is about to descend from the mountaintop of victory at Jericho to the valley of defeat at Ai. Joshua was a gifted and experienced leader, but he was still human and therefore liable to error. In this experience, he teaches us what causes defeat and how we must handle the discouragements of life.

—*Be Strong,* page 101

1. What must it have been like for the Israelites to go from such a miraculous victory at Jericho to a sudden defeat at Ai? What overall lesson did God teach the Israelites through this experience?

More to Consider: The sinner described in Joshua 7:1 is named Achan, or Achar. Not surprisingly, his name means "trouble." Because of Achan's disobedience, Israel was defeated at Ai, and the enemy killed thirty-six Jewish soldiers. But Achan's story isn't unique. Read about Abraham in Genesis 12:10–20; David in 2 Samuel 24; and Jonah in Jonah 1. What do these stories teach us about the damage one person can do outside the will of God?

2. Choose one verse or phrase from Joshua 7—8 that stands out to you. This could be something you're intrigued by, something that makes you uncomfortable, something that puzzles you, something that resonates with you, or just something you want to examine further. Write that here.

Going Deeper

From the Commentary

Like every good commander, Joshua surveyed the situation before he planned his strategy (Num. 21:32; Prov. 20:18; 24:6). His mistake wasn't in sending out the spies but in assuming that the Lord was pleased with His people and would give them victory over Ai. He and his officers were walking by sight and not by faith. Spiritual leaders must constantly seek the Lord's face and determine what His will is for each new challenge. Had Joshua called a prayer meeting, the Lord would have informed him that there was sin in the camp, and Joshua could have dealt with it. This would have saved the lives of thirty-six soldiers and spared Israel a humiliating defeat.

It's impossible for us to enter into Joshua's mind and fully understand his thinking. No doubt the impressive victory at Jericho had given Joshua and his army a great deal of self-confidence, and self-confidence can lead to presumption. Since Ai was a smaller city than Jericho, victory seemed inevitable from the human point of view. But instead of seeking the mind of the Lord, Joshua accepted the counsel of his spies, and this led to defeat. He would later repeat this mistake in his dealings with the Gibeonites (Josh. 9).

—*Be Strong,* pages 104–5

3. Review Joshua 7:2–5. In what ways did Joshua walk by sight and not by faith? Why shouldn't he have assumed God would give his men victory? What steps did he miss in preparing for the battle?

From the Commentary

Since Israel had sinned, Israel had to deal with its sin. God told Joshua that the nation had stolen that which belonged to Him and had hidden it among their own possessions as if it were theirs.… The nation had been sanctified in preparation for crossing the Jordan (3:5), but now they had to be sanctified to discover an enemy in the camp. They had to present themselves to God so He could expose the guilty man.

What the Lord said to Joshua helps us see Achan's sin (and Israel's sin) from the divine point of view. What they did was *sin* (7:11), a word that means "to miss the mark." God wants His people to be holy and obedient, but they missed the mark and fell short of God's standard. It was also *transgression* (v. 11), which means "to cross over." God had drawn a line and told them not to cross it, but they had violated His covenant and crossed the line.

—*Be Strong,* page 108

4. Underline the occurrences of the word *accursed* (or *devoted [to destruction]*) in Joshua 7:6–15. What does this term mean? Why the emphasis on this theme? Does it seem like overkill? Why or why not? What message was God giving to the Israelites through this word?

From the Commentary

The phrase "Give glory to God" was a form of official oath in Israel (John 9:24 NIV). Achan had not only sinned against his own people, but he had also grievously sinned against the Lord, and he had to confess his sin to Him. When he said "I have sinned," he joined the ranks of seven other men in Scripture who made the same confession, some more than once, and some without sincerity: Pharaoh (Ex. 9:27; 10:16), Balaam (Num. 22:34), King Saul (1 Sam. 15:24, 30; 26:21), David (2 Sam. 12:13;

24:10, 17; Ps. 51:4), Shimei (2 Sam. 19:20), Judas (Matt. 27:4), and the Prodigal Son (Luke 15:18, 21).

—*Be Strong,* pages 109–10

5. Read the Scripture passages noted above. How do each of these confessions compare to Achan's? How can you tell which were sincere and which were insincere? Why would a sincere confession matter in Achan's story? What does this teach us about the role of confession in the life of an individual believer? In a community?

From the Commentary

Since a law in Israel prohibited innocent family members from being punished for the sins of their relatives (Deut. 24:16), Achan's family must have been guilty of assisting him in his sin. His household was judged the same way Israel would deal with a Jewish city that had turned to idols. Achan and his family had turned from the true and living God and had given their hearts to that which God had said was accursed—silver, gold, and an expensive garment. It wasn't worth it!

At the beginning of a new period in Bible history, God sometimes revealed His wrath against sin in some dramatic way. After the tabernacle had been set up, Nadab and Abihu invaded its holy precincts contrary to God's law, and God killed them. This was a warning to the priests not to treat God's sanctuary carelessly (Lev. 10). When David sought to restore the ark to its place of honor, and Uzzah touched the ark to steady it, God killed Uzzah (2 Sam. 6:1–11), another warning from God not to treat sacred things carelessly. At the beginning of the church age, when Ananias and Sapphira lied to God and God's people, the Lord killed them (Acts 5:1–11).

—*Be Strong,* page 110

6. Review Joshua 7:24–26. Why do you think God responded to Achan's sin in this manner? What message was He giving to the Israelites? Why do you think God chooses to use such dramatic events in key points of His people's history? (See other examples in the *Be Strong* excerpt above.)

More to Consider: Read Isaiah 65:10 and Hosea 2:15. How does God reframe the "valley of Achor" in these passages? What message does this give us about how God can turn sorrow into hope?

From the Commentary

Once the nation of Israel had judged the sin that had defiled their camp, God was free to speak to them in mercy and direct them in their conquest of the land. "The steps of a good man are ordered by the LORD, and He delights in his way. Though he fall, he shall not be utterly cast down; for the LORD upholds him with His hand" (Ps. 37:23–24 NKJV). No matter what mistakes we may make, the worst mistake of all is not to try again; for "the victorious Christian life is a series of new beginnings" (Alexander Whyte).

You start with the Word of God. We today don't hear God's audible voice as people often did in Bible times, but we have the Word of God before us and the Spirit of God within us, and God will direct us if we wait patiently before Him.

—*Be Strong,* page 116

7. Respond to this statement in light of Joshua 8:1–2: "No matter what mistakes we may make, the worst mistake of all is not to try again." How did the Israelites try again? How did God provide second chances for them? How does God give us second chances today?

From the Commentary

God is not only the God of new beginnings, but He's also the God of *infinite variety*. Remember the words of King Arthur that I quoted in chapter 2? "And God fulfills himself in many ways, / Lest one good custom should corrupt the world." God changes His leaders lest we start trusting flesh and blood instead of trusting the Lord, and He changes His methods lest we start depending on our personal experience instead of on His divine promises.

The strategy God gave Joshua for taking Ai was almost opposite the strategy He used at Jericho. The Jericho operation involved a week of marches that were carried on openly in the daylight. The attack on Ai involved a covert night operation that prepared the way for the daylight assault. The whole army was united at Jericho, but Joshua divided the army for the attack on Ai. God performed a mighty miracle at Jericho when He caused the walls to fall down flat, but there was no such miracle at Ai. Joshua and his men simply obeyed God's instructions by setting an ambush and luring the people of Ai out of their city, and the Lord gave them the victory.

It's important that we seek God's will *for each undertaking* so that we don't depend on past victories as we plan for the future.

—*Be Strong,* pages 117–18

8. Why did Joshua initially depend on past victories when he tried to defeat Ai? How does past success affect the way people view future challenges? What does God's infinite variety teach us about His nature? About the role of constantly seeking His will? How do we go about doing that?

From the Commentary

> When morning dawned, the king of Ai saw the army of Israel positioned before the city, ready to attack. Confident of victory, he led his men out of the city and against the Jews. "They are the most in danger," said Matthew Henry, "who are least aware of it." Joshua and his men began to flee, and this gave the men of Ai even more assurance of victory.
>
> According to Joshua 8:17, the men of Bethel were also involved in the attack, but no details are given. Whether they were already in Ai or arrived on the scene just in time, we aren't told, but their participation led to the defeat of their city (12:16) as well as Ai.
>
> —*Be Strong*, pages 119–20

9. What causes nations (and their leaders) to become overconfident about their strength or safety? What leads to overconfidence in individuals' lives? How can we find the proper balance of confidence and caution?

From the Commentary

> At some time following the victory at Ai, Joshua led the people thirty miles north to Shechem, which lies in the valley between Mount Ebal and Mount Gerizim. Here the nation obeyed what Moses had commanded them to do in his farewell speech (Deut. 27:1–8). Joshua interrupted the military activities to give Israel the opportunity to make a new commitment to the authority of Jehovah as expressed in His law.
>
> —*Be Strong,* page 121

10. Read Moses' farewell speech to the Israelites in Deuteronomy 27:1–8. What was his commission to the people? In what ways do the Israelites follow through with his wishes? (See Josh. 8:30–35.)

Looking Inward

Take a moment to reflect on all that you've explored thus far in this study of Joshua 7—8. Review your notes and answers and think about how each of these things matters in your life today.

Tips for Small Groups: To get the most out of this section, form pairs or trios and have group members take turns answering these questions. Be honest and as open as you can in this discussion, but most of all, be encouraging and supportive of others. Be sensitive to those who are going through particularly difficult times and don't press for people to speak if they're uncomfortable doing so.

11. When have you walked by sight and not by faith? How did that go? What prompted your faithless approach to the situation? How might it have played out differently had you sought faith first?

12. God turned a place of sorrow into one of hope (the valley of Achor). How has God turned your sorrows into hope? How have you grown closer to God in this process?

13. Have you ever fallen prey to overconfidence when you should have been cautious? Describe that situation. Why were you overconfident? What was a positive reason for your confidence? What did you miss that could have saved you from failing? Is overconfidence always a sign of having missed God's will? Explain.

Going Forward

14. Think of one or two things you have learned that you'd like to work on in the coming week. Remember that this is all about quality, not quantity. It's better to work on one specific area of life and do it well than to work on many and do so poorly (or to be so overwhelmed that you simply don't try).

Do you want to practice trusting God to lead you in uncertain times? Be specific. Go back through Joshua 7—8 and put a star next to the phrase or verse that is most encouraging to you. Consider memorizing this verse.

Real-Life Application Ideas: In Joshua 7—8, we learn about the dangers of trusting the past instead of continually seeking God's will. Take stock of your own faith life. Are there areas in your life where you tend to trust "what has always been" instead of regularly seeking God's will? Perhaps there are long-established patterns that you take for granted. Look closely at your habits and behaviors and the way you relate to others. If you find areas where you don't regularly seek God's will, make a determined effort to do so right away (and henceforth).

Seeking Help

15. Write a prayer below (or simply pray one in silence), inviting God to work on your mind and heart in those areas you've noted above. Be honest about your desires and fears.

Notes for Small Groups:

- *Look for ways to put into practice the things you wrote in the Going Forward section. Talk with other group members about your ideas and commit to being accountable to one another.*

- *During the coming week, ask the Holy Spirit to continue to reveal truth to you from what you've read and studied.*

- *Before you start the next lesson, read Joshua 9—12. For more in-depth lesson preparation, read chapter 9, "We Have Met the Enemy and He Is Our Neighbor," in* Be Strong.

The Mistake of Nothing
(JOSHUA 9—12)

Before you begin ...
- *Pray for the Holy Spirit to reveal truth and wisdom as you go through this lesson.*
- *Read Joshua 9—12. This lesson references chapter 9 in* Be Strong. *It will be helpful for you to have your Bible and a copy of the commentary available as you work through this lesson.*

Getting Started

From the Commentary

> An anonymous wit reminds us that a dentist's mistake is pulled out, a lawyer's mistake is imprisoned, a teacher's mistake is failed, a printer's mistake is corrected, a pharmacist's mistake is buried, a postman's mistake is forwarded, and an electrician's mistake could be shocking. The novelist Joseph Conrad wrote, "It's only those who do nothing that make no mistakes."
>
> —*Be Strong,* page 129

1. What was Joshua's mistake in chapters 9—12? What prompted his mistake? What were the ramifications of his mistake?

2. Choose one verse or phrase from Joshua 9—12 that stands out to you. This could be something you're intrigued by, something that makes you uncomfortable, something that puzzles you, something that resonates with you, or just something you want to examine further. Write that here.

Going Deeper

From the Commentary

> While Israel was at Mount Ebal and Mount Gerizim, reaffirming their commitment to the Lord, the kings in Canaan were getting ready to attack. They had heard about the defeat of Jericho and Ai and were not about to

give up without a fight. It was time for them to go on the offensive and attack these Jewish invaders. The city-states in Canaan were not always friendly with one another, but local rivals can often come together when they have a common enemy (Ps. 2:1–2; Luke 23:12).

After an experience of great blessing, God's people must be especially prepared to confront the enemy, for like Canaan, the Christian life is "a land of hills and valleys" (Deut. 11:11). But Israel's greatest danger wasn't the confederation of the armies of Canaan. It was a group of men from Gibeon who were about to enter the camp and deceive Joshua and the princes of Israel. Satan sometimes comes as a devouring lion (1 Peter 5:8) and sometimes as a deceiving serpent (2 Cor. 11:3), and we must be alert and protected by the spiritual armor God has provided for us (Eph. 6:10–18).

—*Be Strong*, pages 129–30

3. Review Joshua 9:1–15. Why should God's people prepare to confront the enemy after a great blessing? Does this seem like a pessimistic view of life? Why or why not? What makes this a wise view? What does this tell us about the enemy? About diligence?

From the Commentary

> The Gibeonites assembled a group of men and equipped
> them to look like an official delegation from a foreign city.
> Their clothing, food, and equipment were all designed to
> give the impression that they had been on a long and dif-
> ficult journey from a distant city. Satan is a counterfeiter
> and "masquerades as an angel of light" (2 Cor. 11:14 NIV).
> He has his "false apostles" and "deceitful workmen" (v. 13
> NIV) at work in this world, blinding the lost and seeking
> to lead believers astray. It's much easier for us to identify
> the lion when he's roaring than to detect the serpent when
> he's slithering into our lives.
>
> —*Be Strong,* page 130

4. Why did the Israelites buy the Gibeonites' deception? How should they
have acted? In some ways, the Israelites' welcoming of the Gibeonites
seemed like a generous and kind act. Why was it wrong of them to be so
welcoming? What lessons does this have for us today?

More to Consider: Read John 8:44. How do the Gibeonites prove this truth? What is the motivation for their lies?

From the History Books

No matter what your opinion of the war in Iraq, one thing appears certain: The United States had gathered bad intel about the purported weapons of mass destruction. Armed with confidence that their sources were telling the truth, the military marched in to find and dispose of weapons that could have caused great harm to neighboring nations. But when the inspectors arrived, they found little to support the claim of such weapons. While it's possible the weapons were well hidden (or disposed of) prior to the inspectors' arrival, it's more likely that the United States was acting on bad information.

5. How did lies or deception hurt the United States in this scenario? What risks did the United States take when choosing to act on the intelligence they received? How were they like or unlike the Israelites who trusted the Gibeonites' words? What lessons can we glean from both of these stories to better respond to threats or perceived threats, both nationally and personally?

From the Commentary

> Joshua and the princes of Israel were impetuous and didn't take time to consult the Lord. They walked by sight and not by faith. After listening to the strangers' speech and examining the evidence, Joshua and his leaders concluded that the men were telling the truth. The leaders of Israel took the "scientific approach" instead of the "spiritual approach." They depended on their own senses, examined the "facts," discussed the matter, and agreed in their conclusion. It was all very logical and convincing, but it was all wrong. They had made the same mistake at Ai (Josh. 7) and hadn't yet learned to wait on the Lord and seek His direction.

> —*Be Strong,* pages 131–32

6. Is the "scientific" approach to examining a situation always wrong? Why or why not? How could the Israelites have tempered (or tested) their "by sight" analysis with a spiritual approach? How can churches do this today?

From the Commentary

> True faith involves exercising patience (Heb. 6:12).
> "Whoever believes will not act hastily" (Isa. 28:16 NKJV).
> Moses had told the Jews, "Be careful not to make a treaty
> with those who live in the land where you are going, or
> they will be a snare among you" (Ex. 34:12 NIV). But in
> their haste Joshua and the Jewish leaders broke God's law
> and made a covenant with the enemy. Since their oath
> was sworn in the name of the Lord (Josh. 9:18), it could
> not be broken. Joshua and the princes of Israel had sworn
> to their own hurt (Ps. 15:4; Eccl. 5:1–7), and there was no
> way to revoke their oath or be released from their promise.
>
> —*Be Strong,* pages 132–33

7. What were the practical results of the oath the Israelites made with the
Gibeonites? Why couldn't they have reneged on the oath? In what ways
are God's people today living in the enemy's territory? What "oaths" do
we sometimes make with the enemy? How can we avoid making the same
mistakes again and again?

From the Commentary

How did the leaders of Israel discover that they had made a big mistake? Knowing that they were now out of danger, perhaps the "ambassadors" openly admitted what they had done. Or maybe the Gibeonites were overheard rejoicing in their success. Did some of Joshua's spies return to camp after reconnaissance and recognize the enemy? Perhaps the Gibeonites overheard the plans for Israel's next attack and had to inform the leaders that a solemn oath now protected those cities. However it happened, Joshua discovered that he and the princes had blundered, and no doubt they were humbled and embarrassed because of it.

We must give the leaders credit for being men of their word. To violate their oath would have been to take the holy name of Jehovah in vain, and this would have brought about divine judgment. Years later King Saul violated this oath, and God judged the nation severely (2 Sam. 21). Military leaders of lesser character than Joshua might have argued that "all's fair in love and war" and forced the Gibeonites to divulge information that would help him conquer their city. Instead, when the Jewish army arrived at Gibeon and the neighboring cities, they didn't attack them.

—Be Strong, pages 133–34

8. Review Joshua 9:16–27. Why did the Jewish people grumble at what their leaders had done? Why was keeping the oath so important to Joshua and the leaders? What does this say about their leadership?

From the Commentary

> When you make agreements with the enemy, expect to end up paying a price and having to defend them in order to protect yourself. This is why God's people must remain separated from the world (2 Cor. 6:14–18). I wonder whether Paul had Joshua in mind when he wrote, "No one engaged in warfare entangles himself with the affairs of this life, that he may please him who enlisted him as a soldier" (2 Tim. 2:4 NKJV).
>
> —*Be Strong,* page 135

9. Review Joshua 10:1–28. How is this story an example of the message in 2 Corinthians 6:14–18? What are some aspects of modern society that tempt leaders and churches to make "agreements" with the enemy? What's the difference between learning to work within a culture and giving in to it?

From the Commentary

Joshua's words in 10:25 must have thrilled the hearts of his brave soldiers. They echo the words God spoke to him when he began his career (1:6–9). Since Joshua is a type of Jesus Christ, we can apply this scene and these words to Christ and His people. Jesus has defeated all His enemies and will one day return and destroy them forever. No matter how they may rage and rebel (Ps. 2:1–3), our Lord's enemies are only the footstool at His feet (Ps. 110:1; 1 Cor. 15:25). Through Him, we can claim victory and put our feet on the necks of our enemies (Rom. 16:20).

—*Be Strong,* pages 139–40

10. What warnings can we take from the story of Joshua and the Gibeonites? What encouragement can we take from the story? What does this story teach us about how God works with our mistakes?

Looking Inward

Take a moment to reflect on all that you've explored thus far in this study of Joshua 9—12. Review your notes and answers and think about how each of these things matters in your life today.

Tips for Small Groups: To get the most out of this section, form pairs or trios and have group members take turns answering these questions. Be honest and as open as you can in this discussion, but most of all, be encouraging and supportive of others. Be sensitive to those who are going through particularly difficult times and don't press for people to speak if they're uncomfortable doing so.

11. Describe a time when you should have acted but chose not to act. What prompted your inaction? How did fear play into that? Ignorance? What actions should you have taken? How might the story have played out differently if you'd sought God's will for the circumstance?

12. Think of a time when you trusted someone was telling the truth, only to discover later he or she was lying. How did that make you feel? How did it affect the way you later interacted with that person? How was this like and unlike the situation the Israelites faced with the Gibeonites? How does

a living, breathing faith help you make wise decisions in circumstances like this? How do you cultivate that living, breathing faith?

13. The Israelites had to keep the oath they made with the Gibeonites. The consequences of their rash decision were significant. What are some of the consequences you've had to endure from rash decisions? How do you reclaim your relationship with God when you've broken it due to poor decision making?

Going Forward

14. Think of one or two things you have learned that you'd like to work on in the coming week. Remember that this is all about quality, not quantity. It's better to work on one specific area of life and do it well than to work on many and do poorly (or to be so overwhelmed that you simply don't try).

Do you need to learn how to walk by faith instead of sight? Be specific. Go back through Joshua 9—12 and put a star next to the phrase or verse that is most encouraging to you. Consider memorizing this verse.

Real-Life Application Ideas: Think about promises you've made that may or may not have been wise decisions at the time. Have you kept these promises? If not, why? Why is it important to keep the promises you make? When is it right to break a promise? Take stock of the promises you're trying to keep and set them before God, asking Him for wisdom both in how to keep the promise and what you're supposed to learn from it. Then make a commitment to seek God's will before making any promises or oaths in the future.

Seeking Help

15. Write a prayer below (or simply pray one in silence), inviting God to work on your mind and heart in those areas you've noted above. Be honest about your desires and fears.

Notes for Small Groups:

- *Look for ways to put into practice the things you wrote in the Going Forward section. Talk with other group members about your ideas and commit to being accountable to one another.*

- *During the coming week, ask the Holy Spirit to continue to reveal truth to you from what you've read and studied.*

- *Before you start the next lesson, read Joshua 13—21. For more in-depth lesson preparation, read chapter 10, "This Land Is Our Land!" in* Be Strong.

Dividing Lines
(JOSHUA 13—21)

Before you begin …
- *Pray for the Holy Spirit to reveal truth and wisdom as you go through this lesson.*
- *Read Joshua 13—21. This lesson references chapter 10 in* Be Strong. *It will be helpful for you to have your Bible and a copy of the commentary available as you work through this lesson.*

Getting Started

From the Commentary

Joshua had successfully completed the first half of his divine commission: He had conquered the enemy and was in control of the land and the cities (1:1–5). Now he had to fulfill the second part of that commission and divide the land so that each tribe could claim their inheritance and enjoy what God had given them (v. 6). (See Num. 34—35.)

—*Be Strong*, page 145

1. Which half of the divine commission do you think was more daunting for Joshua? What unique challenges would he face with the dividing of the land?

More to Consider: The word inheritance *is found over fifty times in these nine chapters. Why is this such an important theme here? What does this say about the Israelites and their relationship with their God?*

2. Choose one verse or phrase from Joshua 13—21 that stands out to you. This could be something you're intrigued by, something that makes you uncomfortable, something that puzzles you, something that resonates with you, or just something you want to examine further. Write that here.

Going Deeper

From the Commentary

> The Jews *inherited* their land. They didn't *win* their land
> as spoils of battle or *purchase* their land as in a business
> transaction. The Lord, who was the sole owner, leased the
> land to them. "The land must not be sold permanently,"
> the Lord had instructed them, "because the land is mine
> and you are but aliens and my tenants" (Lev. 25:23 NIV).
> Imagine having God for your landlord!
>
> —*Be Strong,* page 145

3. Why is it significant that the Israelites inherited their land rather than winning it as spoils? What was the "rent" God asked of His people? What did God promise in return? (See Lev. 26 and Deut. 27—30.)

From the Commentary

> Throughout the conquest of Canaan, Gilgal had been
> the center of operations for Israel. Later, Joshua moved

the camp and the tabernacle to a more central location at Shiloh (18:1).

We don't know Joshua's exact age at this time in Israel's history, although he could well have been a hundred. Caleb was eighty-five (14:10), and it's likely that Joshua was the older of the two. Joshua lived to be 110 (24:29), and the events described in the last half of the book could well have taken over ten years.

The system for assigning the territories in Canaan is given in 14:1–2. Eleazar the high priest, Joshua, and one representative from each of the tribes (Num. 34:13–29) cast lots before the Lord and in this way determined His will (Prov. 16:33). When Joshua relocated the camp at Shiloh, they changed the system (Josh. 18:1–7).

—Be Strong, page 146

4. What does it mean to "cast lots" before the Lord? Why is this system used to determine the distribution of land? What challenges might Joshua face in this process?

From the Commentary

> Reuben, Gad, and the half tribe of Manasseh had agreed to help the other tribes conquer the land before they returned to the east side of the Jordan to enjoy their inheritance (Num. 32). They had asked for this land outside the boundaries of Canaan because it was especially suited to the raising of cattle. The fact that these two and a half tribes would not be living within God's appointed land didn't seem to worry them. Moses graciously agreed to their choice and let them settle across the Jordan. When we study the twenty-second chapter of Joshua, we'll learn that while their choice may have been good for their cattle, it created serious problems for their children.
>
> —*Be Strong*, page 147

5. Review Joshua 13:1–33. Why would any of the tribes choose land outside of Canaan? What risks were they taking on by this request? (See Josh. 20—22.) What does this say about their priorities? Why did Moses agree to such a request?

From the Commentary

> Four times in these chapters, we are reminded that the
> Levites were given no inheritance in the land (Josh. 13:14,
> 33; 14:3–4; 18:7), because the Lord was their inheritance
> (Deut. 18:1–8; 10:8–9; Num. 18). The priests received
> certain portions from the sacrifices as their due, and both
> the priests and Levites shared in the special tithes and
> offerings that the people were commanded to bring.
>
> —*Be Strong*, page 148

6. What other factors might have contributed to the decision to scatter the
tribe of Levi? What were the Levites' primary responsibilities? How might
tribal responsibilities have affected their ability to serve God and teach
God's people the Law?

From the Commentary

> The next tribes to be settled were Judah in the south
> (14:6—15:63), Ephraim across the middle of the land

(16:1–10), and the other half of Manasseh in the north (17:1–18).

Since Caleb belonged to the tribe of Judah and had been one of the two faithful spies, he received his inheritance first (Num. 13:30). Joshua, the other faithful spy, was the last to receive his inheritance (Josh. 19:49–51). Caleb reminded his friend Joshua of the promise Moses had made to them forty-five years before…. This promise gave Joshua and Caleb joy and courage as they endured years of wandering and waiting.

—Be Strong, page 148

7. Read Numbers 14:24, 30 and Deuteronomy 1:34–36. What promises did Moses give Joshua and Caleb? How were these promises fulfilled? Read Ephesians 1:3–19 and 1 Peter 1:3–6. What do these verses tell us about our inheritance today? How do we claim this inheritance?

From the Commentary

Caleb was eighty-five years old, but he didn't look for an easy task, suited to an "old man." He asked Joshua for mountains to climb and giants to conquer! His strength was in the Lord, and he knew that God would never fail him. The secret of Caleb's life is found in a phrase that's repeated six times in Scripture: "He wholly followed the LORD God of Israel" (Josh. 14:14; also see Num. 14:24; 32:12; Deut. 1:36; Josh. 14:8–9). Caleb was an overcomer because he had faith in the Lord (1 John 5:4).

—*Be Strong*, page 149

8. What does it say about Caleb that he continued to seek challenges even in his old age? How can his life serve as an inspiration for believers today?

More to Consider: Traditionally in the nation of Israel the sons inherit property from their parents, but the daughters of Zelophehad saw to it that they weren't discriminated against (Josh. 17:3–6; Num. 27:1–11). Why is this significant in the biblical narrative?

From the Commentary

Seven tribes still had to have their inheritance marked out for them, and apparently they were slow to respond to the challenge. Unlike Caleb and the daughters of Zelophehad, these tribes didn't have faith and spiritual zeal. These tribes had helped fight battles and defeat the enemy, but now they hesitated to claim their inheritance and enjoy the land God had given them. "The lazy man does not roast what he took in hunting, but diligence is man's precious possession" (Prov. 12:27 NKJV).

At this point, Joshua and the leaders inaugurated a new system for allocating the land. After each of the seven tribes appointed three men, all twenty-one men went through the remaining territories and listed the cities and the landmarks, describing each part of the land. They brought this information back to Joshua, who then assigned the various portions to the remaining seven tribes by casting lots before the Lord.

—*Be Strong,* page 152

9. Why would any of the tribes have hesitated to claim their inheritance? What fears might they have been harboring? Why then did Joshua devise a new system for divvying up the land? What does this entire section of Joshua teach us about how we're to respond to God's generous gift of our inheritance?

From the Commentary

> This long section in the book of Joshua (21:1–45) closes
> with three wonderful affirmations:
>
> First, God was faithful and gave Israel the land (Josh.
> 21:43). He kept the covenant that He made, first with
> Abraham (Gen. 12:7) and then with his descendants.
>
> Second, God gave Israel victory over all their enemies and
> then gave them the rest from war (Josh. 21:44; see 1:13, 15;
> 11:23). What the ten unbelieving spies at Kadesh Barnea
> said could never happen *did* happen, because Joshua and
> the people believed God and obeyed His Word.
>
> Third, God kept His promises (21:45). At the close of
> his life Joshua would remind the people of this (23:14),
> and Solomon reminded them of it when he dedicated the
> temple (1 Kings 8:56).
>
> —*Be Strong*, pages 156–57

10. After forty years of wandering, the Israelites finally found their God-
promised home. How might they have received the affirmations Joshua
gave at the end of this section? How can we receive these same affirmations
today?

Looking Inward

Take a moment to reflect on all that you've explored thus far in this study of Joshua 13—21. Review your notes and answers and think about how each of these things matters in your life today.

Tips for Small Groups: To get the most out of this section, form pairs or trios and have group members take turns answering these questions. Be honest and as open as you can in this discussion, but most of all, be encouraging and supportive of others. Be sensitive to those who are going through particularly difficult times and don't press for people to speak if they're uncomfortable doing so.

11. How might you have reacted to the allocation of land as described in Joshua? Do you have a tendency to be thankful for whatever you have, or do you often wish you had more? How does humility factor into our acceptance of God's generosity? What gifts from God are you most thankful for?

12. In what ways have you sometimes been a "borderline believer"— someone who would rather live outside the Promised Land than accept God's gifts? What leads to a "borderline believer" attitude? How do you

find your way back into the Promised Land? What attitudes or behaviors or habits help you to stay in the middle of God's will?

13. Caleb didn't retire when he got older—he asked God for more challenges. Do you welcome challenges or shy away from them? What do you hope the future holds for you? What would it take for you to be as bold as Caleb? Is everyone cut out to be so bold? Why or why not?

Going Forward

14. Think of one or two things you have learned that you'd like to work on in the coming week. Remember that this is all about quality, not quantity. It's better to work on one specific area of life and do it well than to work on many and do poorly (or to be so overwhelmed that you simply don't try).

Do you want to take steps to accept your inheritance from God? Be specific. Go back through Joshua 13—21 and put a star next to the phrase or verse that is most encouraging to you. Consider memorizing this verse.

Real-Life Application Ideas: One of the notable revelations in this section of Joshua is that the Levites didn't get their own land—that they were instead told to travel between lands to be "salt and light" to God's people. Think about the lands you inhabit—at home, work, school, or anywhere else. In what ways are you like the Levites? How are you currently being salt and light in these various "lands"? Think of specific things you can do to be that salt and light wherever you spend time. Then do those things.

Seeking Help

15. Write a prayer below (or simply pray one in silence), inviting God to work on your mind and heart in those areas you've noted above. Be honest about your desires and fears.

Notes for Small Groups:

- *Look for ways to put into practice the things you wrote in the Going Forward section. Talk with other group members about your ideas and commit to being accountable to one another.*

- *During the coming week, ask the Holy Spirit to continue to reveal truth to you from what you've read and studied.*

- *Before you start the next lesson, read Joshua 22—24. For more in-depth lesson preparation, read chapters 11 and 12, "And When the Battle's Over" and "The Way of All the Earth," in* Be Strong.

Home
(JOSHUA 22—24)

Before you begin …
- *Pray for the Holy Spirit to reveal truth and wisdom as you go through this lesson.*
- *Read Joshua 22—24. This lesson references chapters 11–12 in* Be Strong. *It will be helpful for you to have your Bible and a copy of the commentary available as you work through this lesson.*

Getting Started

From the Commentary

"In defeat unbeatable; in victory unbearable." That's the way Sir Winston Churchill described a British army officer famous in the Second World War. The first half of the description would apply to Joshua, because he knew how to win victory out of defeat. But the last half doesn't apply at all; for as commander of the Lord's army, Joshua was magnanimous in the way he treated his troops after the victory. An Italian proverb says, "It's the blood of the soldier that makes the general great." But this general made his soldiers great! This is clearly seen in the way he discharged the tribes who lived on the east side of the Jordan.

—*Be Strong*, page 162

1. Review Joshua 22:1–8. How did Joshua treat the tribes after the battle was over? Why do people tend to be unbearable after victory? What sin crops up with success? What lessons can we glean from Joshua's treatment of others after victory?

2. Choose one verse or phrase from Joshua 22—24 that stands out to you. This could be something you're intrigued by, something that makes you uncomfortable, something that puzzles you, something that resonates with you, or just something you want to examine further. Write that here.

Going Deeper

From the Commentary

> Having fulfilled their mission and kept their promise, the tribes were now free to go home, for God had given His people rest. The concept of *rest* is important in the book of Joshua and means much more than simply the end of the war. The word carries with it the meaning of both *victory* and *security,* and it involved Israel having their "resting place" in the land.
>
> —*Be Strong,* pages 162–63

3. Read Exodus 33:14; Deuteronomy 12:9–10; 25:19; Joshua 1:13–15; 11:23; 14:15; 21:44; 22:4; 23:1. What do these verses tell us about the importance of "rest" to God's people? Where in Joshua 22—24 do we see evidence of God giving His people rest?

More to Consider: Review Hebrews 3 and 4. What do these chapters teach us about the spiritual application of rest for God's people today?

From the Commentary

> Like any good leader, Joshua was more concerned about the spiritual walk of his people than anything else. The army had experienced victory in Canaan because Joshua loved the Lord and obeyed His Word (1:7–8), and that would be the "open secret" of Israel's continued peace and prosperity. Just as they had been diligent in battle, obeying their commander, so they must be diligent in worship, obeying the Lord their God. This was the promise each of the tribes made to the Lord at Mount Gerizim and Mount Ebal.
>
> —*Be Strong,* page 163

4. Why was Joshua concerned about the people's spiritual walk? Where do we see this concern in Joshua 22? What does this teach us about the proper motive for obedience?

From the Commentary

> There's no question that Canaan was God's appointed land for His people; anything short of Canaan wasn't what He wanted for them. The two and a half tribes made their decision, not on the basis of spiritual values, but on the basis of material gain, for the land east of the Jordan was ideal for raising cattle. I'm reminded of the decision Lot made when he pitched his tent toward Sodom (Gen. 13:10–11). In both instances, the people walked by sight and not by faith.
>
> —*Be Strong,* page 165

5. In what ways did the people of Reuben, Gad, and Manasseh divide the nation by their decision? How did they separate themselves from the blessings of Canaan? What did they miss out on by this decision? Who are today's "borderline believers"?

From the Commentary

> The word traveled quickly that the tribes east of the Jordan had erected an altar. While these Transjordanic tribes had been very sincere in what they did, their action was misunderstood, and the other tribes prepared for possible war. But wisely, they waited while an official delegation investigated what was going on. "He who answers a matter before he hears it, it is folly and shame to him" (Prov. 18:13 NKJV).
>
> —*Be Strong,* page 166

6. Why did the news of an altar concern the tribes in Canaan? What could have happened if they acted on rumor instead of investigating the truth? Why do people tend to believe rumors? How do rumors and misinformation contribute to wars? To conflict of any kind? What is the proper way to deal with unsubstantiated rumors?

From the Commentary

> Joshua was about to go "the way of all the earth" (Josh.
> 23:14), the way you and I must go if the Lord doesn't
> return first. But at the end of a long and full life, Joshua's
> greatest concern wasn't himself. His greatest concern was
> his people and their relationship to the Lord. He didn't
> want to leave until he had challenged them once again
> to love the Lord and keep His commandments. His life's
> work would be in vain if they failed to keep the covenant
> and enjoy the blessings of the Promised Land.
>
> —*Be Strong*, page 175

7. How did Joshua prepare his people for the time when he would no longer
be around? (Review Josh. 23—24.) Why was this important to Joshua?
Why was it important to God's people? What are some practical ways to
apply this wisdom to our own lives and the people we care about?

From the Commentary

> Having assembled the leaders of the nation, Joshua pre-
> sented them with two scenarios: Obey the Lord, and He
> will bless you and keep you in the land; disobey Him, and
> He will judge you and remove you from the land. These
> were the terms of the covenant God had made with Israel
> at Mount Sinai, which Moses had repeated on the Plains
> of Moab, and which Israel had reaffirmed at Mount Ebal
> and Mount Gerizim.
>
> Joshua's emphasis was on possessing the land (23:5)
> and enjoying its blessings (vv. 13, 15–16). While Israel
> had gained control of Canaan, there still remained ter-
> ritory to possess and pockets of resistance to overcome.
> (See 13:1–13; 15:63; 16:10; 17:12–13; 18:3; Judg. 1—2.)
> The task of the tribes wasn't finished! The great danger,
> of course, was that the people of Israel would gradually
> change their attitudes toward the pagan nations around
> them and start accepting their ways and imitating them.
>
> —*Be Strong,* page 176

8. What motives did Joshua give the people for remaining separated and
serving the Lord faithfully? (See Josh. 23:3–16.) Why was it important to
Joshua that the people remain separated? What tasks did they still have
ahead of them? What does it mean to be separated today in a good way?
What are the tasks of the church today?

From the Commentary

> In the April 15, 1978, issue of *Saturday Review*, the late author and editor Norman Cousins called history "a vast early warning system," and philosopher George Santayana said, "Those who cannot remember the past are condemned to repeat it." A knowledge of their roots is very important to the Jews because they are God's chosen people with a destiny to fulfill in this world.
>
> Shechem was the ideal location for this moving farewell address by Israel's great leader. It was at Shechem that God promised Abraham that his descendants would inherit the land (Gen. 12:6–7), and there Jacob built an altar (33:20). Shechem was located between Mount Ebal and Mount Gerizim, where the people of Israel had reaffirmed their commitment to the Lord (Josh. 8:30–35). Shechem was indeed "holy ground" to the Israelites.
>
> *—Be Strong,* page 180

9. Review Joshua 24:1–15. Underline the words *Lord* and *serve* (and any variations) in this section. Why did Joshua mention the Lord so many times? What's the point of his emphasis on serving? What was Joshua trying to prepare the people for with this farewell speech? How are these messages valid for the church today?

From the Commentary

Joshua made it clear that the people of Israel had to make a decision to serve the Lord God of Israel. There could be no neutrality. But if they served the Lord, then they would have to get rid of the false gods that some of them secretly were worshipping. Even after the great experience of the exodus, some of the Jews still sacrificed to the gods of Egypt (Lev. 17:7; Amos 5:25–26; Ezek. 20:6–8; Acts 7:42–43). Jacob had given this same warning to his family (Gen. 35:2), and Samuel would give the same admonition in his day (1 Sam. 7:3ff.).

Joshua wasn't suggesting that the people could choose to worship the false gods of the land and God would accept it, for there was no other option but to serve Jehovah. Being a wise and spiritual man, Joshua knew that everybody must worship something or someone, whether they realize it or not, because humanity is "incurably religious." If the Jews didn't worship the true God, they would end up worshipping the false gods of the wicked nations in Canaan. His point was that *they couldn't do both.*

—*Be Strong,* pages 183–84

10. Why did some of the Israelites still serve false gods even after they had been led out of captivity? What causes people to hang on to bad habits? How did Joshua deal with this issue? What are some of the false gods we still serve today? How might Joshua address us about these old habits?

More to Consider: Moses had named Joshua as his successor, but God didn't tell Joshua to appoint a successor. Why is this significant? Later generations seemed to forget what God had done for Israel, even though Joshua had encouraged them to teach their children of God's role in their history. What happened?

Looking Inward

Take a moment to reflect on all that you've explored thus far in this study of Joshua 22—24. Review your notes and answers and think about how each of these things matters in your life today.

Tips for Small Groups: To get the most out of this section, form pairs or trios and have group members take turns answering these questions. Be honest and as open as you can in this discussion, but most of all, be encouraging and supportive of others. Be sensitive to those who are going through particularly difficult times and don't press for people to speak if they're uncomfortable doing so.

11. How well do you embrace the rest God offers? Is it easy for you to rest in God? Why or why not? What's the difference between godly rest and laziness?

12. One of Joshua's main themes in these chapters is preparing the generations that will follow for a life of faith. What are some ways you're preparing those you care about (family, friends, etc.) for the future? What sort of faith legacy do you want to leave?

13. Some of the Israelites continued to worship idols even after they had seen God work miracles with their delivery out of Egypt and into Canaan. What are some of the old habits you battle from life before knowing Christ? Why do these habits linger? What are you doing to overcome them?

Going Forward

14. Think of one or two things you have learned that you'd like to work on in the coming week. Remember that this is all about quality, not quantity. It's better to work on one specific area of life and do it well than to work on many and do poorly (or to be so overwhelmed that you simply don't try).

Do you want to cut an idol out of your life? Learn how to leave a positive faith legacy? Be specific. Go back through Joshua 22—24 and put a star next to the phrase or verse that is most encouraging to you. Consider memorizing this verse.

Real-Life Application Ideas: Think specifically about the sort of spiritual legacy you want to leave your children (or others you care about). What would that legacy look like? What have you already done to share that legacy? Think of practical ways you can build a positive legacy. This could be anything from simply building your own understanding of faith (through further study and worship) to teaching others at church or elsewhere to writing down your journey so others can learn from it.

Seeking Help

15. Write a prayer below (or simply pray one in silence), inviting God to work on your mind and heart in those areas you've noted above. Be honest about your desires and fears.

Notes for Small Groups:

- *Look for ways to put into practice the things you wrote in the Going Forward section. Talk with other group members about your ideas and commit to being accountable to one another.*

- *During the coming week, ask the Holy Spirit to continue to reveal truth to you from what you've read and studied.*

Summary and Review

Notes for Small Groups: This session is a summary and review of this book. Because of that, it is shorter than the previous lessons. If you are using this in a small-group setting, consider combining this lesson with a time of fellowship or a shared meal.

Before you begin …
- *Pray for the Holy Spirit to reveal truth and wisdom as you go through this lesson.*
- *Briefly review the notes you made in the previous sessions. You will refer back to previous sections throughout this bonus lesson.*

Looking Back

1. Over the past eight lessons, you've examined the book of Joshua. What expectations did you bring to this study? In what ways were those expectations met?

2. What is the most significant personal discovery you've made from this study?

3. What surprised you most about Joshua's leadership style? About the Israelites' response to his leadership? What, if anything, troubled you?

Progress Report

4. Take a few moments to review the Going Forward sections of the previous lessons. How would you rate your progress for each of the things you chose to work on? What adjustments, if any, do you need to make to continue on the path toward spiritual maturity?

5. In what ways have you grown closer to Christ during this study? Take a moment to celebrate those things. Then think of areas where you feel you still need to grow and note those here. Make plans to revisit this study in a few weeks to review your growing faith.

Things to Pray About

6. Joshua is a story of victory and faith. As you reflect on the way the Israelites' faith was tested, ask God to reveal to you those truths that you most need to hear. Revisit the book often and seek the Holy Spirit's guidance to gain a better understanding of what it means to be strong.

7. The messages in Joshua cover a wide variety of topics, including faith, seeking God, patience, accepting God's promises, and sharing faith with future generations. Spend time praying about each of these topics.

8. Whether you've been studying this in a small group or on your own, there are many other Christians working through the very same issues you discovered when examining the book of Joshua. Take time to pray for each of them, that God would reveal truth, that the Holy Spirit would guide you, and that each person might grow in spiritual maturity according to God's will.

A Blessing of Encouragement

Studying the Bible is one of the best ways to learn how to be more like Christ. Thanks for taking this step. In closing, let this blessing precede you and follow you into the next week while you continue to marinate in God's Word:

May God light your path to greater understanding as you review the truths found in the book of Joshua and consider how they can help you grow closer to Christ.

A COMPANION TO WIERSBE'S STUDY ON JOSHUA

With over 4 million volumes in print, these timeless books have provided invaluable insight into the history, meaning, and context of virtually every book of the Bible.

Be Strong (Joshua)
Too often today's church seems resigned to defeat. Based on the book of Joshua, this commentary shares the need for strong believers of purpose, while encouraging us to lead victorious lives.

The "BE" series . . .

For years pastors and lay leaders have embraced Warren W. Wiersbe's very accessible commentary of the Bible through the individual "BE" series. Through the work of David C. Cook Global Mission, the "BE" series is part of a library of books made available to indigenous Christian workers. These are men and women who are called by God to grow the kingdom through their work with the local church worldwide. Here are a few of their remarks as to how Dr. Wiersbe's writings have benefited their ministry.

"Most Christian books I see are priced too high for me . . .
I received a collection that included 12 Wiersbe
commentaries a few months ago and I have
read every one of them.
I use them for my personal devotions every day and they
are incredibly helpful for preparing sermons.
The contribution David C. Cook is making to the
church in India is amazing."
—Pastor E. M. Abraham, Hyderabad, India

not just for North American readers!

"Resources in China are insufficient. I found this 'BE' series
was very good for equipping and preaching . . .
We welcome more copies so that I can distribute them
to all coworkers in the county in our annual training."
—Rev. Wang, Central China

To learn more about David C. Cook Global Mission visit:
www.davidccook.org/global